Prayers
for a
Woman's
Heart

© 2013 by Barbour Publishing, Inc.

Compiled by JoAnne Simmons.

Print ISBN 978-1-62416-712-6

eBook Editions:
Adobe Digital Edition (.epub) 978-1-62836-317-3
Kindle and MobiPocket Edition (.prc) 978-1-62836-318-0

Published by Barbour Publishing, Inc., P.O. Box 719, Uhrichsville, Ohio 44683, www.barbourbooks.com

Our mission is to publish and distribute inspirational products offering exceptional value and biblical encouragement to the masses.

 Member of the
Evangelical Christian
Publishers Association

Printed in the United States of America.

INTRODUCTION

We might not like to admit it, but we women tend to worry. . .and our worries can be so heavy—and so hard to let go of! But God wants us to release them to Him. He wants to take away all our anxiety because He cares so deeply for us. May the prayers in this book help you give everything to God in prayer—and at the same time inspire you to constantly converse with Him, constantly praise Him, and constantly seek His will.

Rejoice always, pray continually,
give thanks in all circumstances;
for this is God's will for you in Christ Jesus.
1 THESSALONIANS 5:16–18 NIV

Dear Lord, as I enter into this quiet time with You, calm my mind, body, and spirit. Take my hand and lead me to Your side. I long to feel Your touch, hear Your voice, and see Your face. Whatever comes to me this day, I know You will be with me, as You are now—within me, above me, beside me. Thank You for strengthening my heart. Thank You for giving me the patience to wait on You.

Heavenly Father, I long for Your peace in my heart. Please take every anxious thread, every tightly pulled knot of uncertainty, sorrow, conflict, and disappointment into Your gentle, loving hands.

Lord, if I trust You for my eternal salvation, why don't I trust You for my daily needs? Instill in me the peace that comes from casting all my cares on You. When all hope seems lost, Lord, be with those who suffer. Help them to never abandon hope, for all things are possible with You.

Father, because of Your blessings, a tiny baby has joined us and made us a family. May Your presence in the midst of our family bless this child throughout the years to come.

I am Your ambassador, Lord,
and every day I try to show Your
love to those who do not know You.
I pray that when the time comes,
You will find me worthy.

Father, when happiness is hard to come by, help me to learn to draw more consistently on Your wellspring of joy. Help me delight in the little gifts You bring my way every day.

Lord, help me to be charitable in all that I do. My acts of charity reflect on You, and I want to bring honor to You at all times.

Lord, this language I speak is so inadequate to tell You what I want to say. I can't begin to find the words to thank You for the successes I have in my life. You are awesome.

Father, I pray You will always be my rock, my salvation. Hear me when I call to You for help, for I know You love me.

Father, don't let me feel social pressure when giving. No matter how much or how little I can give, help me to give joyously.

Dear Lord, sometimes life is so busy that I don't take the time to nurture relationships. Help me make friendship a priority.

Heavenly Father, the world is a frightening place. I look around and see endless opportunities for disaster and tragedy. And yet, I place my trust in Your promise to send Your angels to watch over and guard me. Thank You for Your protection.

Lord, I give all my cares to You and try to walk away, but so often I fail. I begin to fear and doubt. Forgive me, and help me to trust You completely.

Father, when I hear myself belittle my husband or speak to him harshly, remind me that Your standard for marriage is common respect and affection. I have found this man with Your help, and I love him.

I need You, Lord, to lift me up, above all these problems, above my circumstances, above my helplessness. You alone can carry me through this.

Strengthen and equip me, Lord, to stay close to my friend during a time of struggle. By Your power, give me the courage to reach out. Use me to help me meet my friend's needs.

Make my heart perfect, Lord. Take my hand, and give me strength. Be strong for me when I don't measure up. My way to attain a perfect heart is through You, Lord, so don't take Your eyes off me.

This trial I'm going through, Lord, I don't know how to handle. But I am certain of one thing: You can handle it.

Father God, help me to be bold and to reach out to people You want me to get to know. Thank You for providing me with friendships that will grow my faith and give me an opportunity to gain and receive support for the challenges I face. Give me discernment so I know where I belong within Your family.

Lord, in the heat of anger, control my tongue, because what I say then can be as damaging to my soul as it is to my victim's reputation.

Lord, on days when I'm having spiritual struggles, my thoughts become full of discouragement and frustration. I don't like to be so controlled by my emotions. Please give me the strength to be pure in every situation.

Lord, I know bad things will come my way in life, but I am secure in Your love that never fails. I am constantly blessed by Your care and concern. I am so important to You that even the hairs of my head are all numbered.

Lord, there are times when I am so down. And then a friend blesses me, and I think of You. It's because of You and the love that You give that I want to reach out to others. Thank You for blessing my life with friends.

Lord, I often make mistakes on the path of life, losing sight of the trail and calling out for You.

Thank You for finding me, for putting my feet back on the path and leading me home.

Lord, You stand before the throne of Your Father and claim me as Your own, exempt from sin and judgment. Because of Your sacrifice, I am made worthy. Thank You.

Lord, give me wisdom and strength in my instruction to my children. Help me to be firm when I need to be, yet tender and giving as the teaching allows. Guide me in how to show love for You and Your laws.

Search me, God, and know my heart;
test me and know my anxious thoughts.
See if there is any offensive way in me,
and lead me in the way everlasting.

PSALM 139:23–24 NIV

I have hidden your word in my heart
that I might not sin against you.

PSALM 119:11 NIV

"If you are pleased with me, teach me
your ways so I may know you and
continue to find favor with you."

EXODUS 33:13 NIV

Lord, I have been running, running,
running in all different directions, but
I need to run to You now and stay in
Your presence.

Father, I know You blessed me
abundantly in the family You have
given me. Help me not to flaunt them or
to take the credit that belongs to You.

Lord, my life is full of distractions,
and I have too little time to absorb
every sermon the way I should. But You
promise You will come into my heart
and live there if I welcome You. Come
into my heart, Lord Jesus.

You know the hearts of everyone, Lord. At first glance, all I see is outward appearances. I want to be a good judge of character. Help me to be discerning. Make me aware when I am being negatively influenced or manipulated. Teach me what I need to know to be a quality friend, and show me the hearts of my friends.

Lord, teach me to look beyond appearance when I choose my friends or my husband. Help me see beyond beauty—or lack of it.

Father, my daily problems come
and go; yet if I remain steadfast and
dedicated, doing the work You have
given me to do, I am confident that my
reward awaits me. Thank You, Lord.

*Father, I admit that once in a while I
have a temper tantrum, disputing Your
guidance and wanting my own way,
but You have never been wrong. Thank
You for Your love and patience, for I
will always need Your guidance.*

Heavenly Father, I have so much to be thankful for. My list of blessings is never ending. May I never fail to praise You and to thank You for the many blessings You have given to me.

True love is kind, not prideful or self-seeking. Lord, fill me with compassion for my fellow Christians so I might be a godly example of love and understanding. I want to emulate You, Jesus.

Because of Your strength, Lord, I can smile. When I need peace, You strengthen me on the inside. This is where I need You the most. Let me reflect Your strength so that my children will be drawn to You also.

Father, I know that I tend to get focused on the negatives, and sometimes my thoughts are crowded with impatience, envy, anger, or resentment. Please help me focus on You. Fill me with pure thoughts.

Dear God, thank You for my old friends. I'm thankful for their faithful friendship. Thank You for the comfort they give me when the world seems overwhelming. Thank You for the laughter they've brought into my life over the years. I'm glad our friendship will last into eternity.

Lord, when my family is treated unfairly or someone judges me before knowing the whole story, I want to see justice done. Remind me to rely on You for that justice. Only You have the power to set things right once and for all.

Thank You for the times I am humbled, Lord. You are always there— to listen, to forgive, and to heal. Lord, help me to be repentant, to be willing to be brought low. Heal me, Lord.

Lord, You promise me wonderful rewards when I am charitable. But I cannot answer every request made of me, so I count on You to guide me as to where I should invest my efforts in such a way as to bring You glory.

Light makes me feel good, Father.
I love it when the sun comes streaming
through my windows. When the day
ends, I'm glad to be able to turn on
the lights and promote a cheerful
atmosphere in my home. Light offers
hope. That's what I want to do.
I want to draw my children to You.
I want my friends and neighbors and
even people I don't know to see You in
me. Let me be a light for You, Father.

You are like an army, Lord, surrounding me with Your strength and power. I don't have to depend on my limited might and abilities. Teach me to draw on Your strength.

Lord, show me all the good You have done for the faithful throughout history, and give me some of Your strength when my own fails. Let my dependence on You turn weakness into strength.

Father, help me to be diligent in understanding You and Your precepts. Please give me a continuous desire to know You better.

Father, physically, I'm wearing out. But in the core of my being, in my heart, I still feel strengthened by You. What a blessed promise that this inner strength will be my portion forever.

This burden is heavy, Lord. There are days when I don't know how much longer I can go on.

But Your Word says that You will provide a way of escape. You help us carry our burdens. Thank You for Your promise.

Father, many temptations come from evil forces that are so deceptive they are hard to see. The devil fights against us daily. Thank You for providing a way that we can be protected from the full assault of Satan's deceitfulness.

Thank You, Lord, for Your love and faithfulness to us. Thank You for making us Your people and for allowing us to be the sheep of Your pasture. Thank You for allowing us to serve such a great God!

Lord, keep me strong in my faith, no matter what. When I am following You, I can be blessed, no matter what others say about me. Thank You, Jesus, for mapping the way for me and for my children.

Lord, please increase my inner strength. Remind me that although I seem powerless, Your power knows no limits and You will provide whatever strength I need to see me through my current crisis.

Father, help me to be the woman that my family needs. Show me how to love them more.

Lord, help me study Your Word and grow in knowledge of You in order to attain godliness. Then I can help my children understand how to live godly lives.

I know I can trust in You, Lord. Thank You for Your strength that never fails. It is there for all eternity. You don't weaken like I do. You are omnipotent.

Father, when troubles come, I never have to face them alone. Thank You for always being with me as my refuge and strength. When all else fails, I put my trust in You and am never disappointed.

When I am afraid, I put my trust in
you. In God, whose word I praise—
in God I trust and am not afraid.

PSALM 56:3-4 NIV

"I will remember the deeds of the
LORD; yes, I will remember your
miracles of long ago. I will consider
all your works and meditate on
all your mighty deeds."

PSALM 77:11-12 NIV

"You are worthy, our Lord and God, to
receive glory and honor and power, for
you created all things, and by your will
they were created and have their being."

REVELATION 4:11 NIV

Dear God, I am grateful for the friends who participate in both my joys and sorrows. My discouragement is never so overwhelming when my friends help me carry it, and I find meaning even in my life's greatest sorrows. Laughter shared is twice as hilarious, and I take the deepest satisfaction in my life's blessings when I share them with my friends. Thank You for giving us the ability to communicate our feelings to one another; thank You for sending Your Spirit to us through our friends.

Lord, thank You for Your concern for my friends and family members. I know You love them even more than I do.

Lord, I need Your help to learn to appreciate all that life offers, knowing there is profit in both the easy and hard times.

Father, my trials are not major, so far. But I know that things can go wrong in an instant. When I cry to You, I know You hear. Thank You for Your promises and never-ending care.

I've made mistakes, Lord. But someday You will present me faultless, cleansed by Your blood. The evidence of Your power to lift me up and make me whole fills me with exceeding joy. I praise You forever and forever.

Lord, I know there will come a day when we will be in heaven with You. I look forward to that time, and I thank You for the opportunity to share that time and place with You.

When Your purpose is revealed
to me, Father, help me to accept my
responsibility and do Your will.

*Lord, the next time I am angry, guide
me away from sin until I can speak
words of peace and comfort once again.*

Lord, I want my heart to continually
be filled with praise and thanksgiving to
You. Keep me anchored in the thought
that all You do is for my good and
glory. Only You are deserving of my
praise and adoration.

Father, help me to be sensitive to the people around me. When I am tempted to make things all about me, remind me that You created me for friendship. I want to be a better friend. Help me to prefer others to myself. I want to be a better listener so I really hear my friends. I want to help them if I can in the things that concern them. Let my words encourage them. Show me how to strengthen them with Your goodness.

Father, I find it hard to find time to relax. Thank You for making me to lie down even when I don't want to. Thank You for leading me beside quiet waters when I need the solace.

Lord, I seem to be focused on the worldly aspects of life. Change my life, my thoughts, my desires. I want to live a life that is pleasing to You.

Father, I thank You for answers to prayer. It is wonderful to know I have a God who delights in hearing and answering my prayers. I am glad to be able to give thanks.

Lord, let me know when I am wrong. That way I can come to You for cleansing and an opportunity to make things right. Thank You for the truth in Your Word, even though sometimes the truth hurts.

Lord, I pray that my children and their children and each successive generation will understand that all the glory for our many blessings belongs to You. Without You we would be nothing and would have nothing.

Father, I praise You for Your support. When my strength fails, Yours is always sufficient. Thank You for Your constant love and care, for picking out my cry and never failing to rescue me.

Lord, help me to remember that although Your promises are free for the taking, I still need to accept them, claim them, and then live in faith that they are mine.

Lord Jesus, I know that You are my best friend. Teach me to be a true friend to You and others.

In the midst of suffering, I want to keep my eyes on You, Jesus. The suffering You endured for my sake makes my trials look like nothing. Help me look forward to the promise and to forget the temporary troubles I have now.

Father, I welcome Your help.
You know what I need, and I
trust Your provision, knowing You
always act in my best interests and
want me to have a happy life.

Father, it often seems that might makes right and I stand no chance, but I know Your power can overcome whatever evil men might plan. When I am in despair, fill me with faith in Your justice.

I want to be a fruitful vine, Lord.
With Your help I can, whether the
fruit I bring is a cheerful attitude or
money to help provide for my family.
Show me the best way to contribute to
the happiness of my home and family.

Through You, Lord, I can live a life that will give others no right to accuse me of any wrongdoing. I pray that You will allow my life to be an example that will encourage my family, friends, and others to come to You.

Father, my heart is breaking. I need to know that You are near and that You care. Gently remind me that You have the power to heal every hurt, and help me make it through what I'm facing right now.

Father, help me understand
faithfulness and to trust in Your love
above all else, claiming none of Your
glory as a personal reward.

*Father, thanks to You I get to start
over, fresh and clean, because You
have made me a new person. I now
have a lifetime of new days to spend
any way I choose. Thank You for
Your never-ending forgiveness.*

Thank You, Lord, for being
so faithful. Thank You for Your
compassion—that is just the right
amount to get me through the day.

Life is busy, and sometimes I put
the things I need to do to get ahead
before my relationships. Lord, help
me to establish a firm foundation of
loyalty, trust, honesty, and integrity
in my friendships. When our eyes
are on You, we will remain strong in
our commitment to You and to one
another. Help me to discern when I
need to drop a task and be there for my
friends.

I need look no further than You,
Lord, to help me. It is Your name
that I trust. It is Your power that
will help me meet this challenge.

Thank You, Father, for giving us sound doctrine. I have boundaries set by You that I can follow and teach to my children. All we have to do is look to You and Your Word for guidance.

Lord, show me how to be a godly woman, how to have true contentment that comes from service to You. Help me to reinforce in my home the need to be satisfied with doing Your will.

Lord, You've given me a life that abounds with rich blessings, and You've guaranteed that because of this You also have great expectations of me. Help me to be faithful to these expectations.

*Lord, I need deliverance from my anxiety. I am not responsible for everyone and everything—
You are, and I know You are trustworthy. Help me to hope in You and trust Your protection.*

Lord, give me the strength to forgive others so You will forgive me my own trespasses.

*Into your hands I commit my spirit;
deliver me, L*ORD*, my faithful God.*

PSALM 31:5 NIV

*Teach me to do your will, for you
are my God; may your good
Spirit lead me on level ground.*

PSALM 143:10 NIV

L*ORD, you are my God; I will exalt you
and praise your name, for in perfect
faithfulness you have done wonderful
things, things planned long ago.*

ISAIAH 25:1 NIV

Lord, thank You for the blessing of my family. Help me to not only tell them how much I love them each day but to show them as well.

Humble me, Lord. Fill me with the desire to hearken to my parents. I can learn so much from them and benefit from their life experiences. I believe this is Your will. Thank You for Your patience and guidance.

Lord, You welcomed me into Your family with love and acceptance. Help me be as kind to others as You have been to me—cheerfully welcoming everyone.

Lord, remove the fears that bind me
so that I can be happy in the knowledge
that You are there to comfort me—
no matter what else is happening.

*Father God, it seems my cynical
attitude is keeping me from
performing acts of hospitality. Please
give me the faith and strength to do
what needs to be done, not because
I want a reward but because it is an
honor to do Your work.*

Lord, help me be the peacekeeper, never the one who stirs up more anger. Help me be an example to my whole family.

Thank You for dealing with my sins so thoroughly, Lord—for granting me a new start every day and proclaiming that I am worth saving.

Father, help me not to be a complaining woman. Fill my heart with joy over the tasks that I need to get done around the house.

Heavenly Father, we live in a world that lifts up proud people. Make us all aware of how much You value sacrifice. Help us to have the humble spirit we need when we come before You.

Father, give me the courage I need to control my fears. I know that You love me and watch over those I love far better than I can. Strengthen my heart.

Father, help me to learn to be sensitive to the needs of others. Help me to show them Your love in every interaction.

Father, I know the importance of spending quiet time with You in Your Word. Please place in my heart the urgency to be committed to my personal Bible study so that I can grow in You.

Lord, help me to rejoice in the time I have with my family today. I don't want to dwell on what might happen in the future; I want to relish this chance to nurture and cherish the blessings You've given me.

Loving God, remind me to watch for You in daily life. Help me to see You in people, nature, and circumstances.

Father, I long to be a mother. If it is Your will, there will be children. If this is not the path You have chosen for me, I trust in You and know You will make my life meaningful in other ways.

Father, I pray You will always be my rock, my salvation. Hear me when I call to You for help, for I know You love me.

Please protect my children, Lord. I've tried to instill godly values, but I can't be with them all the time. Please send Your Spirit with them. Keep them from being corrupted and led away from Your truth.

God, do not trust in my talents, diligence, money, education, luck, or others to help me meet this challenge. I trust in You.

Lord, keep me on the right path when my own plans are flawed, because only You know where You need me to be today and tomorrow.

Lord, as my children grow, help me to treat them like young trees, planting them firmly in Your Word. Then, as I see them getting stronger every day, I pray that they will trust You and be blessed.

Lord, I'm grateful that I have the opportunity to teach my children the truths that are found in Your Word. I'm trusting that You will open their spiritual understanding. I am looking forward to the day that they will accept You as Savior.

Lord, I know so many parents who don't try to see things through their children's eyes and who are not sympathetic to the trials they face.I don't want to be like that. Help me to be like You, Lord.

Dear Lord, thank You for Your Word. Surround me with people who will pray for me, and place people in my life for whom I can pray. Together let us boldly proclaim Your name.

Father God, the heroes my children admire today have weaknesses. But not You, Lord; You are perfect. Your strength is everlasting. Help my children to trust You as their only hero—the One they can trust forever and ever.

Lord, I can do all things through You! You give me the power! You give me the energy! You give me the ways and the means! Give me the strength I need to accomplish the goals You set before me. Plant the words "I can do all things through God—He strengthens me!" in my heart forever and ever.

Lord, You know my friend's needs and
the desires of her heart. But sometimes
I don't know what to say or how to
pray. Holy Spirit, You are the One
who helps us in our weakness. When
I do not know what to pray for, You
intercede for me with groans that words
cannot express. Search my heart and
intercede for my friend today, Lord. I
pray that Your will would be done.

Lord, help me to remind my children
every day that there is nothing ahead
they need to fear. Because of You and
Your sacrifice, we have victory.

Father, help us to put our past troubles behind us and look forward to the days ahead. Help us to forget some of the things that we have done and said to each other. Our marriage is wounded and bleeding, Lord. We need Your balm of love to heal it. Give us Your special touch so that we may never part. For what You have brought together shall not be put asunder. Give us strength, hope, wisdom, and guidance.

Father, help me to be a godly woman. Show me how to put my relationship with You first.

Father, raising obedient, loving children requires me to show gentleness and patience, not threats or harshness. I pray that You will teach me how to soften each correction with the same love I receive from You.

Still my complaining heart, Lord. Fill me with rejoicing. I want to teach my children patience by my own example. Give me strength for the task.

God, help me to share my life with those around me. Let others see Jesus in the way I live and the way I love.

*Even though I walk through the
darkest valley, I will fear no evil, for
you are with me; your rod and your
staff, they comfort me.*

PSALM 23:4 NIV

*From the ends of the earth I call to you,
I call as my heart grows faint; lead me
to the rock that is higher than I.*

PSALM 61:2 NIV

*May God be gracious to us and bless us
and make his face shine on us—so that
your ways may be known on earth,
your salvation among all nations.*

PSALM 67:1–2 NIV

Lord, thank You for the ability to work—at home and on the job. Let everything I do be praise to You.

Put a new song in my mouth, Lord. Let others see me being patient and waiting on You, no matter what difficulty I'm facing. Help them learn the same song of joy that You are giving me.

Lord, help me to be understanding with my children, to encourage rather than discourage. I want to take their hands and walk with them, as You've taken time to walk with me.

Thank You, Lord, that in Your perfect plan You've seen fit to give me beautiful children whom I probably don't deserve. Thank You for allowing me to be a mother. That is truly a gift from You.

Dear Lord, thank You for the special memories I've created with my friends . . .for little moments in my day when those "remember when's" creep into my thoughts and leave a lasting smile.

Heavenly Father, thank You for faithful friends, and thank You for Jesus, the most faithful Friend of all.

Lord, my spouse and I have been through such trials, yet each time we make it over a hurdle together, our love grows stronger. Continue to help us through the trials of this life. And in all things, may we praise Your name for the wonders and joys of marital love.

Lord, I'm grateful that I can show my children where to turn in times of trouble. They don't have to try to do it all themselves, because we are all Your children.

Lord, please give me the strength and the wisdom to be the godly example that my children need to see. I know that the life I live will have a profound influence on the attitudes my children develop concerning You.

Be with all women living alone, Lord. Be their faithful companion and guide as they struggle to build a life based on Your love and care.

Father, thank You for my friends. Help me to be a friend that is always ready to help others.

I often feel that I lack faith, Lord, that You must be speaking promises for someone else—someone more faithful and deserving of them. Show me the error of this thinking.

Father, when it comes to money matters, I cannot approach perfection, but I know with Your help I can learn to handle our family finances faithfully.

As I read Your Word, it is a constant reminder of Your love for me. It also reminds me of how much You love my kids and that You have their best interests at heart.

Father, You gave me my children to cherish, and that includes being gentle with them. I do treasure them, Lord, so help me to impart Your gentleness to them.

Lord, I want to be instrumental in helping my family establish a close walk with You. Direct me daily to renew my commitment to follow in Your steps. Thank You for being the example I need.

Father, when the time comes for me to release my children into Your care, give me the courage to do so graciously.

Lord, I have watched my friends carry burdens that humanly speaking should be unbearable. Yet with these trials You give them incredible joy. I praise You for all You are!

Father, I ask for Your wisdom and guidance. Instruct me in the best ways to teach my children about Your great love. I trust You will guide me.

Father, Your Word contains the best parenting instruction and advice I could ever possess. Give me the wisdom to weigh everything else I read against what the Bible says. Thank You for leading me in right paths.

Lord, thank You for asking Jesus to pay the high price for what I've done. The thought of His sacrifice and Your unending grace humbles me beyond words. "Thank You" will never be enough.

Lord, we are a hurt nation—an angry nation struggling to maintain its values while still dealing firmly with those who hate us. Guide our nation's leaders during these difficult times. We trust in You and long for peace.

Lord, I appreciate friends who accept me for who I am and encourage me to grow in my relationship with You. They want to see me succeed in every area of my life. They are there for me when I need them, concerned for my life just as I am for theirs. Thank You for giving me the courage to be open and truthful with them. You have joined our hearts together with Your love.

Father, help me to love my friends enough to lovingly share the Gospel with them.

I don't mean to take advantage of others, but I've done it. Forgive me for it. Jesus, open my eyes to see that I hurt my friends when I'm late, cancel, or just don't show up. Let me see this before it's too late to keep my commitments. Teach me how to schedule for interruptions and still keep the appointments that are most important on the schedule.

Examine my heart and my mind,
heavenly Father. Show me anything
that I need to make right with You.

Father God, the joy has gone out
of my life. I need Your reassurance
that You will never give me a burden
without helping me bear it. Be my
strong hope of a better future.

Whenever I feel pressure to exalt
myself above others, Lord, remind me
that my worth is found in You alone.
Teach me to serve, to love, to be honest,
to put the needs of others first—
to live a humble but blessed life.

I can't believe it, Father. I really messed up this time, and my friend still forgave me. I didn't really expect her to ever want to speak to me again, but she hugged me and told me we'd just start again. That felt so wonderful! Thank You for friends who forgive.

Give me discernment, Lord,
as to when I should speak
and when I should keep quiet.

Lord, help me to live according to Your guidelines and show my kids that Your plan is best as they strive to live for You.

Holy Spirit, I cannot live life on
my own strength. I ask that You
would come and fill me with
Your presence. Empower me with
discernment to make better life choices,
and give me energy to thrive—not just
survive. Give me a heart to seek You
and serve others. Pour into my life
more love, joy, peace, and patience—
to be a good friend, a wise worker—
a woman who is blessed, Lord.

I know there are many things I cannot control, no matter how hard I may try, and many of life's events break my heart. Still I have hope, because through it all I have You. Thank You, Lord, for hope.

I tell You my problems and You listen, Lord. I speak of the good things in my life and You smile. I ask You for advice, knowing it will come in Your time. I am no longer lonely; I am loved.

O Father, You have draped me in the garments of salvation and wrapped me snugly in the robe of righteousness. I am beautifully adorned by You—for You. You have given me all I need to live a joyful life, and I rejoice in Your gifts of beauty.

Lord God, I put my hope in You for the situations I am in, for the hurts that afflict me, and for each second of my future. I trust in You that You will raise me up, just as You did Jesus.

*How abundant are the good things
that you have stored up for those who
fear you, that you bestow in the sight
of all, on those who take refuge in you.*

PSALM 31:19 NIV

*Send me your light and your faithful
care, let them lead me; let them
bring me to your holy mountain,
to the place where you dwell.*

PSALM 43:3 NIV

*You are my strength, I watch for you;
you, God, are my fortress, my God on
whom I can rely. God will go before me.*

PSALM 59:9–10 NIV

You don't just notice me and pass on—You actually take the time to think about me, pay attention to me, help me when I need help, and protect me when I need protecting. I am not alone. I am not forsaken. Thank You, Lord.

You love the impaired, those who struggle with life and sometimes go under. You love me, Lord, so much that You call me forth by name and beautify me with Your salvation, the most precious ornament I could ever wish for.

Lord, help me not to be quick to judge or oppose love between others. Let me give love time to do its work. I may never see the result I want, but I am sure it is in Your hands.

Lord, time passes so quickly. Yet for this precious amount of time I have here on earth, I want to enjoy life with my spouse. He is so dear to me. Let Your love flow through me and into my other half.

Jesus, thank You for forgiveness. I know I'm not worthy of the grace You offer me every day. Please help me to never take Your gift for granted.

Father, please be the center of my marriage. Let our love be strong in You.

Father, be with us today, and stay near as we strive to raise our family in a way that will please You and allow us to accomplish whatever You have planned.

Lord, I believe the call to motherhood comes from You. Help me approach my calling with a meek and humble spirit. Only when my outlook becomes Christlike will I truly be considered worthy of this calling.

Father, help me to cast my cares on You, knowing that You will sustain me.

Father, vows to You must be honored. Help us to keep our marriage vows and allow our love to grow strong.

Lord, help me teach all our children about You, about Your great promises, and about the peace that I pray will be their inheritance.

Dear Lord, I know that not everyone I meet has Your purposes in mind. As I venture out, help me to seek Christian friendships and stay safe in everything that I do.

Jesus, please bring new opportunities for God-filled relationships into my life today. I want You to use me to bless others and bring them closer to You.

Lord, help us to remember that You love us and You are faithful to all of Your promises.

Lord, help me give my family the aid and support they need.

Father, I need rest—rest from my schedule, rest from the demands of my family, rest from "doing" to a place of simply "being." Lead me to that place. Calm my mind and my emotions so I can slow down enough to find real rest.

I've messed up again. I can hardly forgive myself. But when my foot slips, Your mercy holds me up! Forgive my offenses, Lord. Take away this feeling of anxiety within me. Help me to stop belittling and berating myself. My confidence is so low. Comfort my soul with Your presence, Your love, Your Spirit. And as You keep forgiving me, help me to forgive others.

O Lord, You alone are our refuge and strength. Help me to direct my friends to come to You first in a crisis.

Father, I want my children to know what I expect of them and then obey. Give me guidance to establish the right reward and discipline system. I need strength in that area, Lord.

Father, teach me Your ways
so that I can know You
and find favor with You.

Lord, I can see Your inner power at work in my children as they grow in You. Your Spirit inside us is a life-changing power that will always be available to us wherever we are. Thank You for this wonderful gift.

Lord, I ask for Your help in raising my children. May Your patience and kindness be made visible through my actions.

Lord, surround me with friends who know You and Your Word. Surround me in a crisis so I can still hear Your voice of wisdom and reason.

Father, thank You for all You have given me, for all You have taught me, and for all the good times still to come.

Lord, You told me to give and that if I do, it shall be given to me. You don't say what "it" is, but Your generosity is unmatched, and Your blessings are always wonderful. Thank You!

Father, You have given us Your Word and Your Holy Spirit to teach us. Help me to seek You each day.

Lord, You are made strong in my weaknesses. I need Your help to remember that and to teach my children that we should count it all joy when we are faced with trials and suffering.

Lord, help me to put aside my needs, to draw my child close, and to assure him of my love and, more importantly, of Your love.

Thank You, Lord, for what I do have, which is happiness. Help me to be wise with what money I have and use it in a way that pleases You.

Thank You, Jesus, for the example You have set for a true friend. Help me to be a better friend as I follow You.

Heavenly Father, I want my children to serve You, but I know they can only do that if they have true faith in You. Help me live so that they will want this kind of faith.

I am so mad at myself. I have been doing wrong and hiding it from everyone. I even imagined I could hide it from You, but You know all. Lord, please forgive me for not admitting my sins to You. Help me to do better. I don't want to live this way. Give me Your never-ending mercy and eternal loving-kindness.

Father, there are certain children whom I do not want to let into my house because of bad behavior. Show me how I can help guide them in some small way without taking over their parents' duties.

Lord, I need Your gentle wisdom for every area of life. I'm so thankful that what You offer is the best.

I know my children have a lot to teach me, Lord. Help me to be receptive to Your lessons, especially when You send them through a child.

Thank You for granting my request and blessing me with a beautiful family. I give my children back to You. I ask that You would use each one for Your glory.

Dear God, be with my friends even when we can't be together. Thank You that miles have no meaning in eternity.

Lord, I want to obey You in everything and also lead my children to obey You. Through our obedience to You, help us to reach many people for Your kingdom.

Lord, help me to redefine "greatness" for my children and show them worthy examples of those who have received You. They need to know that there is a better, more glorious way to live.

Lord, give me a new heart. Empty this heart of stone, the one so easily offended. Fill it with Your love.

Lord, make me a living sacrifice for You, that I might lead others to You. Let my praises be a godly example in my home. I praise You with all that is within me.

*Do not remember the sins of my
youth and my rebellious ways;
according to your love remember me,
for you, LORD, are good.*

PSALM 25:7 NIV

*Your ways, God, are holy. What god is
as great as our God? You are the God
who performs miracles; you display
your power among the peoples.*

PSALM 77:13–14 NIV

*Your promises have been
thoroughly tested; that is
why I love them so much.*

PSALM 119:140 NLT

I don't know why, Lord, but I just keep bringing up old offenses and throwing them into the faces of those who have hurt me. I know that's not how You want me to behave. If I keep on this course, there's no telling how many people I will alienate from my life. Help me to forgive others and not remind them of past misdeeds. Help me to pour out Your love to all.

Thank You, God, for Your Word.
It instructs me how to live.
It brings joy to my days and gives
me strength when I am weak.

Give me the strength of Your forgiveness this morning, Lord. Help me to love and not hate the person who has hurt me. Thank You for releasing the poison of unforgiveness that has been building up within me.

Father, help me see when my children need gentle, loving correction, and show me the best approach. Let me be as kind and patient with my children as You are with me.

I know that death comes to us all, Lord, but sometimes I feel I cannot give up a loved one. In time of loss, send me Your comfort and peace, I pray.

I acknowledge that You, Lord, are the giver of all good gifts, and I thank You for Your provision in my friendships.

Father, please give me the wisdom I need to properly advise my children. Help me teach them to seek guidance from Your Word and live in communion with the Holy Spirit.

Lord, I humbly ask that You would forgive me for any ways I have hurt my friend. Help me to deal with things I'm aware of, and bring to my mind the things I'm not. Please give me the courage and faith to forgive my friend when she hurts me. I know that all my wrongdoings are forgiven by You when I confess them. May I be a person who in turn forgives others.

Lord, I want to become less so that You can become more. I am Your servant— help me to serve productively and creatively. All, Lord, to Your honor!

Lord, I'm ashamed to admit that sometimes I have a hard time taking You at Your Word. Please show me how to trust You more, even when my mind can't grasp it and my heart can't accept it.

Lord, when I am old, I want my children to respect and love me. By my actions toward others, I am always teaching—either respect or disrespect. I want to set the right example for my children as I honor older people.

Lord, help me to show compassion
for my children and also for strangers.
You were the best example. You loved
everyone, Lord. Help me do the same,
and in doing so set an example for my
children.

*I want my life to be a sacrifice for You,
Lord. Help me live a life of praise for
You before my children. Guide me in
showing my children how to make
the sacrifice of praise to You.*

Jesus. What a wonderful name! It is
the only name we need to call upon
for salvation. I praise You for being the
Way, the Truth, and the Life, Lord.

Lord, I am human and often tempted.
Be with me when I am tempted, and
show me the true joys of self-control.

Heavenly Father, help me show my
children the way to You while they
are so eager to learn. I want to teach
them about Your grace and mercy—the
wonderful gifts You have made available
to everyone.

Lord, I have been so lonely lately—I need more friends. In Your graciousness, please provide for my need for companionship. It's hard to start again, to find someone who cares and makes the time for a new person in her life. But You are the giver of good things, and I trust that You will bring the right people at the right time.

I lift my soul to You, and I trust in You, Lord. Show me Your ways, and teach me Your paths.

No matter what my friends are facing, Father, give me the patience to stand with them, no matter how long it takes. Even when things that concern them don't seem all that important to me, remind me that they would be there for me if I needed them. Help me to remember them in my prayers, and remind me that my relationships with them are centered in our faith in You.

Lord, keep Yourself in the forefront of my mind this morning and throughout this day. You are the One I worship and the One I serve.

Lord, You are my strength and my song. Help me teach my children to sing, no matter what is going on around us. I want us to make a joyful noise to You, Jesus, the Author and Finisher of our faith.

Father, I get discouraged when I don't know which way to go. Remind me that You are right behind me, telling me which way to turn. Help me to be quiet and listen for Your guidance.

Lord, I ask in Jesus' name that my unsaved friend would come to know You as her personal Savior. I pray for her salvation and for her growth in faith. As You reveal Yourself to her, may she come to truly experience You—not just in her head, but in her heart. Draw her closer to You, Lord, so she may feel the power of Your presence. Revive her spirit, Lord, for her sake and Your glory.

Father, quite often I
pray for what is impossible.
But for You, nothing is impossible.

Thank You, Father, for giving us
all the things we need for life and
godliness. You are the Great Provider.

*Lord, I praise You for Your unshakable
loyalty to me. Help me to be loyal not
only to You but also to my family,
friends, church, and my employer.*

Lord, thank You for the gifts You've
bestowed on me. Help me find
moments to enjoy them and share them
with those I love.

Father, Your Holy Spirit is telling me that self-control is not one of my strengths, and I need to work on it. I need temperance. Help me turn things over to You and allow You to develop self-control in my life.

Lord, I really want to grow spiritually. I need to—for my own daily walk with You and, more importantly, because You've commanded me to. Thank You for giving me the strength to fulfill Your commands and to grow spiritually.

*I will give thanks to you, Lord,
with all my heart; I will tell of all your
wonderful deeds. I will be glad and
rejoice in you; I will sing the praises
of your name, O Most High.*

PSALM 9:1–2 NIV

*Taste and see that the Lord is good.
Oh, the joys of those who take refuge
in him! Fear the Lord, you his godly
people, for those who fear him will
have all they need.*

PSALM 34:8–9 NLT

*Have mercy on me, O God, according
to your unfailing love; according to
your great compassion blot out my
transgressions. . . . Wash me, and I
will be whiter than snow.*

PSALM 51:1, 7 NIV

Father, direct me in how to be involved in the lives of my children. Help me build on Your teachings by setting the right example, praying for them, being there for them, and caring for them.

Dear Lord, help me choose friends who will encourage me to do right, and help me be that kind of friend.

Father, help me to remember that my children's suffering is every bit as real to them as mine is to me. I need to be compassionate, to show them that they will experience exceeding joy because of these trials.

Father, I want to make You exciting and interesting to my children. Give me creative ideas as we take walks, clean the house, do schoolwork, or engage in other routine activities. I pray it will be a delight for all of us.

Lord, I feel so gloomy today.
In my sadness, help me to remember
that even when I'm down, I can
choose to put my hope in You. Instead
of telling myself lies that push me
deeper into despair, I can look to
Your truth. Remind me of the good
things You have done in the past.
I choose to praise You.

Father, cleanse me from my ungrounded fears. Fill me with confidence. You are the strong Protector. I am thankful that, because of Jesus, we will be lifted up as the stones in a crown.

Lord, help me to draw my children close when that's needed and to become involved in their play when that would be better. Mold me into the mother they need.

Lord, help me focus on relationships and cultivate authentic friendships. Help me invite my friends into my life as it is, rather than orchestrating impressions.

Heavenly Father, I pray that my children will love Your Word and understand how special they are to You and that You have something for each of them to meditate on each day.

Lord Jesus, draw my family close to You. Fill our home with Your presence and our lives with Your love. Help each one of us to realize the importance of blessing others.

Father, let Your love fill my heart so that it pours over and floods the children You have so graciously given me. Help me show them how special they are to me.

In all my prayers for those I know,
Father, may I have a heart of joy. Bless
my family and friends. Bless those who
need You today. May I find satisfaction
in lifting up prayers for others.

*Lord, help me to teach my children
that to grow as encouragers they can
start with small things as they comfort
others, and build from there.*

Father, show me the way to true
forgiveness. I want to do Your will
despite my weakness. Be my guide along
this difficult path that leads to my own
sorely needed forgiveness.

Lord, give me confidence in Your promises so I may never worry about the welfare of my children, whom You love even more than I do and have promised to care for.

Father, thank You for all the times my friends forgive me. I never seem to use up their forgiveness; thank You for showing Your own nature through them.

Father, thank You for helping us to raise children who appreciate what they have and who work hard to build their own lives, with or without financial riches.

Lord, I have done many foolish things—and I am sorry. I have made unwise choices, and I have been taken captive by the passions and pleasures of the world. Forgive me. Thank You for saving me by Your mercy and a love that's hard to fathom. Sometimes Your kindness startles me. In spite of all I have done wrong, You bring me back to Your good graces. Thank You, gracious Lord.

Lord, as my parents age and need more help from me, remind me that other help is available. You have provided these helpers for us; let us use them wisely.

Lord, look into my life and search my heart. Is there anything hurtful that I have been doing? Remove the sin and selfishness. Help me to stop focusing on how others should change. Lord, cleanse my heart first. I can't change anyone else, so I ask You to show me what needs to go from my life, what needs to stay, and how I can be right with You.

Lord, no matter what happens to upset us on the surface, You are in our innermost being, bringing peace and comfort. Thank You that we can always trust You.

Lord, You've given me plenty of instruction on parenting, and it's because You know what's best. Thank You for seeing the need to include parenting in Your Word.

Jonathan and David. . . What an incredible pair of friends, Father! Jonathan's willingness to take risks on David's behalf is unbelievable, especially considering that he knew David would be king in his place. Lord, that's the kind of friend I want to be.

Father, thank You for granting
my request and blessing me with a
beautiful family. My prayer now is that
each of my children would accept You
as their personal Savior. Then I ask that
You would use each one for Your glory.

There is no condemnation for us when
we believe in You, Jesus. The covering
of Your blood helps us to prevail
over anything. We never need to
fear anymore. Thank You for
giving us this victory.

O God, help me think before I speak.
Put words of kindness in my mouth
that will build up others instead of
destroying them. I desire to be virtuous.

You defend me, You love me, You lead
me. How great is that! How great are
You! Too wonderful for words. This
morning in Your presence, I rejoice.
This morning, I direct my prayers to
You, knowing that You will hear my
words and interpret my groans. I am
directing my voice to You, Lord, and
patiently await Your instructions.

Lord, I ask that my husband and I would value each other. As he loves me, help me to respect him. As I value him, help him to cherish me. Draw us always closer to You and to each other.

Lord, when I first considered starting a family, I thought I would be a perfect parent. It was easier dreamed than done. I know I need Your assistance if I'm going to be a good mother. I'm so grateful for Your guidance.

Lord, I know You hear my voice when
I pray to You! You are my Strength
and my Shield. When my heart trusts
in You, I am overjoyed. You give me
courage to meet the challenges of the
day. You give me strength to do the
tasks You have set before me. You build
me up, raise me to the heights, and
lead me to places I would never have
dreamed possible. You are the Friend
who will never leave me, the Guide who
walks before me. With You in my life,
Lord, I can do anything.

For your unfailing love is as high as
the heavens. Your faithfulness reaches
to the clouds. Be exalted, O God, above
the highest heavens. May your glory
shine over all the earth.

PSALM 57:10–11 NLT

Yes, my soul, find rest in God; my hope
comes from him. Truly he is my rock
and my salvation; he is my fortress,
I will not be shaken.

PSALM 62:5–6 NIV

Jesus looked at them intently and said,
"Humanly speaking, it is impossible.
But not with God. Everything is
possible with God."

MARK 10:27 NLT

Father, I don't know how You will use my life, but I have faith in Your promises and am always ready to do Your will.

Lord, show me how to be a godly woman, how to have true contentment that comes from service to You. Help me to reinforce in my home the need to be satisfied with doing Your will.

Lord, give me the resolve to make things better, to ignore my pride, and to do whatever is needed to restore the harmony in my family.

Lord, I praise and thank You for bringing into my life people I can call "family"—beyond those to whom I am related. I cherish my friends, the family of believers, and all those other people in my life who are like family to me. Keep us close and connected. Help our relationships to be loving and encouraging. Give me grace, Lord, to treat my brothers and sisters as I, myself, would like to be treated.

Lord, restore our hope in You today.

Lord, my Pilot and my Guide, give me
direction this day. You teach me what
is best for me and direct me in the way
I should go. When I pay attention to
Your commands, You give me peace like
a river. It is to Your living water that I
run. Help me, Lord, to obey You in all
I say and do. Give me the wisdom to
abide in Your Word, all to Your glory!

*Gracious Father, I thank You
for the work I have. May I do
it in a way that is pleasing to
You and that reflects Your glory.*

Dear God, thank You for all my faithful friends. Their understanding, their forgiveness, their love all help me comprehend Your love a little more. Thank You for showing me Yourself through them. May they see You in me.

There's no mistaking, Lord. You've made it clear that I'm to be joyful in each and every task. The next time I'm tempted to complain about the mounds of work, remind me to turn the murmuring into praise.

This is the day that You have made,
Lord! I will rejoice and be glad in it!
Lord, I feel Your light shining upon
me. I feel Your presence all around
me. I glory in Your touch! No matter
what comes against me today, I know
that You will be with me, so there is
no reason to be afraid. All I have to do
is reach for You and You are here with
me. You are so good to me. Thank You,
Lord, for Your goodness and Your love.

Lord, I thank You for Your guidance and protection day after day. Although I never know what the day will bring, You have a plan, and I trust in You.

God, sometimes life is so messy. Nothing has been going right. All I want to do is throw up my hands in frustration. But that is not of You. You are not a God of disorder but a God of peace. Help me to be at peace now as I come to You in prayer. Help me to rest in Your presence and gain Your strength to meet the challenges of this day.

Father, Your guidance is trustworthy. You are our Good Shepherd. You lead us to places of rest when we need them. My children and I need that rest. Thank You for Your leading.

Lord, I ask for Your help when it comes to getting along with my family members. Teach me to focus on the good times we've had together, not the bad, and to concentrate on their good points for the sake of family peace.

Jesus, I want to be a persuasive representative for You to my family and friends. Direct my speech so I can effectively convey to them how You can change their lives like You have changed mine.

God, I long for Your presence and Your touch. Deliver me from worry, fear, and distress. Bind me with Your love and forgiveness as I rest in You. Fill me with Your power and Your strength to meet the challenges of this day. Thank You, Lord, for the way You are working in my life. Keep me close to You throughout this day.

Father, praising You and rejoicing in You must be high on my priority list. Proclaiming Your love to others must never be lacking in my life. Thank You that I am able to rejoice in You!

Lord, it seems that these days I can't get enough rest. I seem to be always on the run. Calm my heart and my soul. I come seeking Your peace, resting in Your arms. Lead me to Your Word, and give me the rest I need.

Dear God, thank You for my friends.
Help me not to take them for granted.
Sometimes my priorities get twisted up
so easily; I start thinking that money
and possessions are more important
than people. Your Son's life shows me
that You treasure individuals far more
than You care about earthly prestige
or power or wealth. Remind me often
how poor my life would be without the
friends You have given me. Help me to
enrich their lives as they have mine.

You are my lamp, O Lord; the Lord turns my darkness into light. With your help I can advance against a troop; with my God I can scale a wall.

Lord, as I dwell on this earth, I feel Your presence beside me. I remember the times You've taken care of me, suffered with me, and led me through the darkness. Remain with me now and for the rest of this day, giving me courage and strength as I trust in You.

Lord, there's so much chaos. Quiet my spirit. Let me close my eyes for a moment and experience Your touch. My strength comes from You, not from any other source. Calm me. Keep me anchored in You and Your Spirit.

It's my faith in You, Jesus, that keeps me sane and gives me peace. I am eternally grateful for that peace, and I thank You.

Thank You, Lord, for being so faithful. Thank You for Your compassion—that it is just the right amount to get me through the day.

Lord, I praise You today for all You have done for me. You have brought help, hope, healing, and restoration, and I want to tell people! Help me proclaim Your goodness, sharing the amazing ways You have come through for me. But as I speak, help me to be a good listener, too.

Thank You, Jesus, for calling sinners to repentance. If You had come only for the righteous, I would not have been called, for I am a sinner. I thank You for Your mercy.

Lord, I come before You to ask that You would establish our home on the solid rock of Your love. Please be our cornerstone. I pray that our family would be rooted in love, grounded in grace, and rich in respect for one another.

Lord, let me be like Abraham, with unwavering faith and belief in Your promises. May I be strengthened by Your Word as I meditate on it before You today, knowing and believing that You have the power to do what You have promised.

God, I don't feel very strong today. In fact, I am filled with that sinking-like-Peter feeling. Buoy my faith, Lord, so that I can stand firm. As I meditate on how You stopped the wind and calmed the sea, how just a touch of Your hand healed others, how there was power even in the hem of Your garment, I know I can stand today, firm in You. Continue filling me with Your power, courage, and strength.

I trust in your unfailing love;
my heart rejoices in your salvation.

PSALM 13:5 NIV

Teach me your way, LORD, that I
may rely on your faithfulness;
give me an undivided heart,
that I may fear your name.

PSALM 86:11 NIV

Because of Christ and our faith in
him, we can now come boldly and
confidently into God's presence.

EPHESIANS 3:12 NLT

Lord, thank You for being with me as
I spend my quiet time in Your presence.
When I am in the wilderness, You tell
me not to fear. You tell me to rise in
Your strength. And then You open my
eyes and direct me to the living water.
Lord, there is no one like You, no one
who loves me as You do. I thirst for
Your presence and am rewarded with
Your peace. Be Thou my eternal fount
of blessing.

Dear Jesus, thank You for loving me even when I fail, encouraging me in my discouragement, and sticking close to me during tough times. May I be as good a friend as You are.

Lord, I believe that You will be with me forever, that You will never leave me nor forsake me, that You will keep my head above the water, and that You love me now and to the end of my days. Thank You for saving my soul and strengthening my faith.

Father, my heart is breaking over the death of someone I love. Fill me with Your comfort and the joy that comes from knowing that when death does come, You will be there to guide us home to You.

Lord, You open the eyes of my heart and fill me with Your awesome resurrection power. As I seek Your face, I am filled with endless hope. I revel in Your glorious riches. I am saved by the power of belief. Enlighten my mind, heart, and spirit as we spend these moments together. I await Your words. Speak to me now!

As I seek to extend the hand of friendship to others, give me wisdom to know which relationships to pursue. Bless me with good friends, Lord.

Jesus, my Jesus, thank You for always being with me, holding me up above the waters of this life, especially when the current is more than I can bear. As You uphold me day by day, my faith grows. There is no one like You, Jesus. No one like You. I am strengthened during this time with You. I overflow with thankfulness and praise. What would I ever do without You in my life?

Father, help me to have patience, knowing my season is coming according to Your timetable and trusting that with Your help, every fruit I produce will be good.

I love You, Lord, and am filled with Your love for me. Words cannot express the glorious joy I feel at this moment, basking in Your morning light, warmed by Your presence at my side. I want You to be with me throughout this entire day. Never leave me. Never forsake me. Give me that faith that believes in things unseen!

Lord, You are my best friend. How could it be anyone else! You are kind, loving, generous, faithful, and giving. You always listen, and You always care. And You have the best advice. But most of all, You laid down Your life for me—for me, Lord! There is no greater expression of love, and for that I am immensely grateful.

Father, protect my family from the evil one today. Help them to keep their focus on You.

Father, teach my husband and
me to work as a team in raising our
children, sharing the good times and
the bad, so that neither of us should be
overburdened.

Lord, I have my own ideas of how
You want me to serve You, to enlarge
Your kingdom here on earth, to
provide for myself, my family, and
my church. But I need Your wisdom.
Which route should I take? When
shall I begin? How shall I go?
Lead me, Lord, into the waters
You have charted for my life.

Father, I can't begin to count the number of times You've wrapped Your loving arms around me and calmed me in the midst of fears. You've drawn me near in times of sorrow and given me assurance when I've faced great disappointment.

Father, when my time on earth comes to an end, I pray I will be able to bear death as well as I bore life, secure in Your love and looking to the salvation that You have promised is mine.

Dear Jesus, I know You are a Friend who sticks closer than a brother, yet sometimes I need the comfort of friends I can see and touch. Help me to say no to extra activities so I have time to invest in friends.

Father, sometimes I have to go against the wishes of others to do Your will, and it's not always pleasant. But Your wishes come before all others, and I will do my best to honor Your name all my days.

Lord, I know that You are the One at work in me; Your Spirit is a part of me, and You guide my thoughts and actions. Thank You for that. I don't know what I would do if I had to live life on my own.

Lord Jesus, help my husband and me to trust and rest in Your unfailing love.

Lord, I want to learn to be patient and trust in You. I know that You will hear my cries and I will be blessed. Thank You for this blessing.

Lord, show me how to be a godly
woman, how to have true contentment
that comes from service to You. Help
me to reinforce in my home the need to
be satisfied with doing Your will.

*Lord, direct me daily to accept and
apply the strength that You have
offered, so that I will truly have the
gentle spirit that You intended me to
have. Thank You, Jesus, that I don't
have to do this on my own.*

Father, on days when I go off on my own, draw me close to You until I calm down and begin to think clearly. Everything is under control. All I need has been provided. Thank You.

God, Your creation is so awesome. Everywhere I look, I see Your handiwork. You have made it all. You have made me. Continue to mold me and shape me into the person You want me to be. Give me knowledge and wisdom in how best to serve You.

Lord, I thank You for the work of Your hands. A wildflower, a mountain scene, the ocean waves on a white-sand beach—the beauty of the earth reveals Your glory. Thank You for the smile of a child, the touch of my beloved's hand, the warmth of our home. I am grateful for the love of friends and meaningful work. You have done great things for us, and we are filled with joy. Thank You for Your many blessings.

Lord, thank You for the amazing grace You show me daily. Help me learn how to extend Your grace in words and deeds to all people.

Lord, You formed all things. And afterward, You invited man to be Your cocreator, allowing him to name things, do things, and serve You. Show me now, Lord, how You want me to employ my talents, my gifts, and myself to make this world a better place. Come to me now, Lord. Imprint upon my mind what You want me to do, which door You want me to walk through.

Dear Lord, be with my friends who don't know You. Help me to plant seeds of faith in their hearts. Let me trust that You will make them grow.

Although I cannot see what the future holds, You see it, Lord. You have it all planned out. Open my ears to Your voice and my eyes to Your creative vision for my life. Help me to see where You want me to go. Then give me the courage to steer my life in that direction.

*Not unto us, O LORD, not unto us,
but unto thy name give glory, for thy
mercy, and for thy truth's sake.*

PSALM 115:1 KJV

*Teach me, LORD, the way of your
decrees, that I may follow it to the
end. Give me understanding, so that
I may keep your law and obey
it with all my heart.*

PSALM 119:33–34 NIV

*May our Lord Jesus Christ himself
and God our Father, who loved us
and by his grace gave us eternal
encouragement and good hope,
encourage your hearts and strengthen
you in every good deed and word.*

2 THESSALONIANS 2:16–17 NIV

Help me, Lord, to focus on You in all I say and do, in every decision I make, and in every direction I take. Help me to make the most of each opportunity. My life's aim is to serve, obey, and seek You. I do not know what to do, but my eyes, Lord, are upon Your heavenly face, and in this I rejoice!

Turn Your ear to us, Father.
Come quickly to our rescue.
Be the rock and refuge of our marriage.

God, grant me the patience, wisdom, and grace I need to be a good listener. Remind me also, Father, to use my words today to lift others up rather than to tear them down.

Lord, may I never hesitate to forgive anyone when You have already forgiven me.

Father, please don't let me fall into the trap of false pride. Whatever small beauty I bring into this world is only a tiny reflection of Your beauty, Your creation, Your perfection.

Forgive me, Lord, for those times when I've doubted Your love. Let me close my eyes, hold out my hand, and know that You are there. Thank You for being with me, Father.

God, You have given me direction. It is time for me to move forward, to sail into unknown waters. You have commanded me to advance. You have already given me the land beyond these seas. All I need to do is sail toward You and take possession of the blessings You have provided. Thank You, God, for allowing me to be a part of Your master plan.

Lord, help me to have wisdom as I pray for the needs of my friends. I want to be an intercessor, to come before You as one who stands in the gap. Whether my friends are hurting or sick or need direction, I am here asking You to help them and heal them. Give them courage and faith in their trials. May Your gracious hand be upon their life.

Father, make me mindful of Your great gifts, that my song may praise Your work in my life.

Lord, You are my hope in an often hopeless world. You are my hope of heaven, my hope of peace, my hope of change, purpose, and unconditional love. Fill the reservoir of my heart to overflowing with the joy that real hope brings.

God, You have known me since the beginning. You know my doubts and fears, yet You love me still. Sometimes I feel as if I am adrift in confusion. I need You to lovingly urge me on past that darkness and into Your light. Thank You for Your patience.

Lord, help me to be as generous to
my family as I am to strangers. Give me
Your guidance. Reveal the needs of my
brother and sister—whether they are
physical, emotional, or spiritual—
and incline my heart to them.

*Heavenly Father, my greatest
responsibility as Your child is to share
the gift of salvation with others. My
family, my neighbors, my children—
so many people need to hear Your
Word. Make me attentive to each
opportunity You present to me.*

Dear God, I was just noticing all the people around me who really could use a friend. For whatever reason, they are alone and hurting. I need to reach out to them. I ask You to give me opportunities and ideas to let them know I care. Let me make the world a little friendlier for them.

You bless my life in many ways every day, Father. May I receive Your blessings with a song of thanksgiving on my lips.

I know what You want me to do, Lord. I hear Your voice telling me how You want me to serve. Help me to put aside my doubts, misgivings, and fears. I want to go where You command. I know You will be by my side through it all.

O Lord, I seek Your wisdom to renew my spirit and help me face the challenges of this life. I believe that You are working in my life and good things await me today. May I further the plans for Your kingdom as You lead me through this life and time.

Dear Lord, please help me to love
with a genuine heart and to take second
place to those around me.

No matter what happens, Lord,
I cannot be separated from You and
Your love. Oh, what that means to me!
Fill me with the love that never ends.
May it flow through me and reach
those I meet this day. May my future
be filled with blessing upon blessing,
and may I praise You today and
in the days to come.

Lord, I don't know if I'll ever understand why You sacrificed Yourself for me. But, from the depths of my being, I want to shout praises to You and tell the whole world what You did for all of us.

Father, help me remember that my priorities are not necessarily the priorities of those I love, so please give me the sense to step back and allow everyone a little leeway to lead their own lives. Help me to be supportive, not bossy.

Lord, sometimes it's easier to give than to receive. I want to be a giver, to take the time to care and help my friends when they need it. And help me to learn to receive, too—so that I'm not too proud to receive generosity from a friend. Give and take, Lord. . .we really do need each other.

Lord, sometimes I have to take a stand, no matter what happens. When these times come, I pray You will give me character and courage.

Father, I need a reminder that what I should be is a servant. I get so wrapped up in the need to maintain order that I forget my job—to meet the needs of my family. Please give me a servant's heart.

God, help me to create a life with You; help me to be not just a lump of clay sitting on a shelf, out of harm's way but unused. Continue to shape me and mold me into the person You want me to be.

Father, help me realize that my wants are temporary and of little importance. Let me lean against You, Lord, relaxed in the knowledge that You will care for me.

No matter what I face today, You, Lord, are going before me. You appear before my very eyes. You will lead me through the desert, sustaining me with Your living water. When I am tired, You will carry me like a child, until I reach the place You have intended for me.

"Stand still and watch the LORD's victory. He is with you, O people of Judah and Jerusalem. Do not be afraid or discouraged. Go out against them tomorrow, for the LORD is with you!"

2 CHRONICLES 20:17 NLT

With the Lord a day is like a thousand years, and a thousand years are like a day. The Lord is not slow in keeping his promise, as some understand slowness. Instead he is patient with you, not wanting anyone to perish, but everyone to come to repentance.

2 PETER 3:8–9 NIV

Father God, thank You for my "heart" friends, my loyal sister friends who listen, care, and encourage me. They are my faithful companions.

Nothing will cause me dismay, nothing will discourage me with You by my side, O Lord of my life. Help me to seek Your advice, Your Word, before I speak, before I move, before I act. Guide me through this maze of life, Lord, with the assurance that You always walk before me. Embed this truth deep within my soul.

When grief comes to me, Father, I know You will understand if I turn my face away from everyone for a time. I know You understand my suffering and long to comfort me.

Do not allow my foot to stumble, Lord. Eliminate the obstacles of worry and fear that line the path before me. Give me hope and courage to face my future. Give me a clear mind to make the right decisions. And, at the end of this day, give me the peace of sweet slumber as I lie down within Your mighty arms.

Dear Father, thank You for watching over me, for meeting all my needs. I am forever grateful for the times You place friends in my life just when I need them most.

Lord, there is so much I do not understand about You. Still, I can see the effects of Your actions, the evidence that You are still active in my daily life. I do not need to physically see You to believe. Your evidence is everywhere.

Lord, thank You for Your gift of physical pleasures, but teach us to use them wisely, according to Your wishes for us. Keep us faithful to our spouses and to Your laws of self-control.

Lord, what a promise You have made to me, that You will supply all I need through Christ. He is my Good Shepherd; with Him I shall not want! Help me to rest confidently in the assurance that in Your time my prayers will be answered.

Lord, I thank You for the joy and privilege of praying for others. What a blessing to be able to intercede, to stand in the gap and move heaven and earth for those I love.

Lord, You know these are hard times. You know how much money this household needs to function each day, week, and month. Hear my prayer and help me to do my part in providing for my family. I thank You for this roof over our heads. And now I humbly beseech You to help us meet our needs.

Father, give me faithfulness in all things, large and small, so that I may be an example to my children and a blessing to my husband—and to all those near me.

I watch and wait expectantly, Lord, for You to answer the petitions I make to You today. I bring them to You, mindful of the way You are always there, ready to listen, ready to advise, ready to answer. Give me the gift of patience as I wait for Your response. Help me not to run ahead of You but to wait and pray and hope.

Lord, teach me to look through appearance when I choose my friends. Help me see beyond beauty—or lack of it.

Dear God, I don't know what lies before me. I feel plagued by the what-ifs that tumble through my mind and pierce my confident spirit. Allow me to let You fill my soul. Help me to be confident in Your wisdom and power to guide me, so that, although You have concealed from me the knowledge of future events, I may be ready for any changes that may come.

Thank You for the work You have given me, Father, with its opportunities to be of service to others and to You. You have made me a woman of value, and my contribution is great.

Lord, sometimes I don't understand why it takes so long for You to answer some of my prayers. At times Your answers are immediate, but on other occasions, I need to keep coming before You, asking over and over again for You to meet my need. Help me to grow during this time. Give me the confidence to ask and keep on asking.

Lord, show me Your way through my difficulties. If my friend does not know You as her Savior, help me lead by example.

Lord, I come to You, thanking You for giving me all that I need each and every day. I have endured some lean times in the past, but right now, things are looking up, and it's all because I looked up—to You! Help me to keep my focus upon You and not on what I lack.

Lord, show me the path to victory every day, because sometimes I find it hard to follow. You know every turn in the road, and I will follow You in security all the days of my life.

I hate being so needy, Lord, so poor, so hurt, so wounded. Troubles plague me every time I try to depend upon myself to meet all my needs. Today I come to You, the Source of all power. Help me to rest assured that You are taking care of me, and that as long as I abide in You, all will be well.

Lord, Your promise of protection gives me a secure feeling. I'm surrounded by Your love and protection. Because You love me and care for me, I can do the same for my children. Thank You for the peace this brings.

God, Your hands created the heavens and the earth. Everything that was created was created through Your Son, Jesus Christ. The trees, the earth, the waters, and the creatures clap their hands in praise to You. This is the day that You have made! I will rejoice and be glad in it as I shout Your name to the heavens!

Lord, help me to be a friend who loves at all times, even when I may not feel like it. Teach me how to love with words—to be encouraging and supportive—and help me to show love by my actions, too. I want to be a better listener, never self-centered. Show me how to bring joy to others in tangible ways, with a phone call, a hug, or a deed that is meaningful to my friend.

I am not worthy of Your gifts of mercy and forgiveness, Father, but I accept them with joy.

Lord, I am so mad! I am angry, and I
need Your help. Why do things have to
go so wrong? I need to do something
with this heated emotion—and I
choose to give You my anger and
bitterness, Lord. Help me be rid of it.
Redeem the confusion, and bring peace
to what seems so out of control. Free
me from resentment and blame. Show
me my part in this conflict as You
speak to the heart of my adversary.
I need Your healing and peace, Lord.

Oh Father, my heart is broken. I no longer have any strength. Fill me with Your power. Put Your arms around me. Let me linger in Your presence, bask in Your love. You are all I need. For without You, I can do nothing. Quench my thirst with Your living water. Feed me with Your bread of life. Nourish me deep within. I come to You in despair. I leave filled with joy.

Lord, help me realize that my understanding is not necessary for the completion of Your plan. You understand everything; all I need to do is have faith.

Lord, I don't need a bunch of yes-women as my friends. Give me relationships with those who care enough to confront. I need Your truth in all my friendships.

Lord, I want to be a more confident woman. I don't want to be afraid of disasters—or just making mistakes. Give me the courage to know that You, Lord, will be my confidence. Let me walk with my head high because I know who I am in Christ: I am Yours!

You go before me and follow me. You place your hand of blessing on my head. Such knowledge is too wonderful for me, too great for me to understand!

PSALM 139:5–6 NLT

Let the morning bring me word of your unfailing love, for I have put my trust in you. Show me the way I should go, for to you I entrust my life.

PSALM 143:8 NIV

Confess your faults one to another, and pray one for another, that ye may be healed. The effectual fervent prayer of a righteous man availeth much.

JAMES 5:16 KJV

Thank You, Lord, for setting the example for me as a parent. There are times when I haven't listened. . .when I've done what I wanted to do, and You chastened me. It hurt, Lord, but I learned a valuable lesson.

Lord, thank You for the joy You bring into my life through simple things. Help me remember that when I look to You, Lord, I can have a more optimistic outlook and be a more positive person. Keep my eyes on You, not on myself or my circumstances, so I can live with a lighter, more joy-filled heart.

Lord Jesus, what a friend You are!
All who know You can look to You in
need. Show me how to be a friend to
others as if I were representing You—not
just because I have to, but because I
see them through Your eyes. Help me
to love my friends at all times, for Your
glory.

*Lord, show my children what
convictions to establish, and
give them the strength to stand
firm in those convictions.*

Thank You for calling me Your friend, Father. Help me to learn Your ways so I can be a better friend to others.

It's a paradox, but it is Your truth—when I am weak, I am strong because Your strength is made perfect in my weakness. Because You are in my life, I can rest in You. With Your loving arms around me, I am buoyed in spirit, soul, and body. When I am with You, there is peace and comfort.

Lord, help me not to judge but to let You decide the fairness of matters. Give me patience—to rest in You and to wait for Your return. I need Your help to teach my children to rest in You, too.

I am feeling so poorly, Lord. You know what is attacking my body. You can see everything. I ask You in prayer, right now, to fill me with Your healing light. Banish the sickness from my body. Fill me with Your presence. Draw me unto You.

Lord, would You please show me how I can reach out to someone who needs a friend? Bring to mind people with whom I can share the love of Christ. Let my words and actions reflect Your love, acceptance, and compassion. Give me eyes to see the needs and a heart to respond.

As I learn to rest in You, Lord, renew me. Give me the ability I need to be patient, no matter what trouble is around me. Let my joyful hope and faithful prayers build up my patience.

Be with all women living alone, Lord. Be their faithful companion and guide as they struggle to build a life based on Your love and care.

Lord, I am reaching out my hand to You, knowing that if I can just touch the hem of Your garment, You will make me whole. I envision You before me. I see the compassion in Your eyes. I know that You love me and that nothing is impossible for You. Fill me with Your love. Give me Your healing touch today.

Father God, thank You for Your Word that shows me how great a friend You are to me and how I can be a good friend to others as well.

Give me the passion, Lord, to serve You with the gifts You have given me. Reignite the enthusiasm I felt when I first began to serve You. Help me to forget about myself and to see only You. Help me to feel Your presence within me. Set me on fire for You and You alone!

I love my children, Lord. I thank You for them, but sometimes I need another person to talk to who understands what I'm going through as a mom. Help me find a friend—someone who needs the kind of companionship I do.

When my time comes to grieve, Lord, be with me. Hold me up with Your mighty arms until I can stand on my own once more. Hasten the passing of my season of grief.

Lord, when I see how You have interceded on my behalf, I want to fall on my face before You. My prayers have been answered in miraculous ways. In times when all I could see was darkness, You provided light and power and hope.

Father, Your correction lasts only a moment, but its blessings are eternal. When I realize You are so concerned for me and want to help me, I am filled with gratitude and am willing to be led in the right direction.

Lord, guide me so that all I am and do will point the way for others, that they also can enjoy the benefits of salvation and join their voices in praise of Your Father in heaven.

Lord, please open my eyes so that I can see how to help others. I know that because of You I have a deep love in my heart for those around me. Show me how to be a blessing to them.

Father, choosing friends isn't always easy. I want to find individuals who share my values and my love for You. Please lead me to the places where I'll be able to find companions who will glorify You.

Lord, in time, I may have to play a more active role in the lives of my aging parents. This can be a difficult time for all of us. I ask for Your help and guidance when this time comes.

Father, help me to be a good friend, a good listener, and a person who offers wise counsel. I pray that I would ultimately turn my friends to You—the One who will never let them down.

Lord, I do not know how to deliver myself from temptation, but You know the way. You have been there. When I stumble, I know Your arms will catch me; if I fall, You bring me to my feet and guide me onward.

Father, when troubles come, I never have to face them alone. Thank You for always being with me as my refuge and strength. When all else fails, I put my trust in You and am never disappointed.

Some days, Lord, I feel as if I am working only to please others. But that's not what it's all about. It is You I am serving, only You. You give me the power to do Your will. It's from You that I receive my reward for a job well done. Thank You for opportunities to serve You and You alone!

"For I know the plans I have for you,"
declares the LORD, "plans to prosper
you and not to harm you, plans to give
you hope and a future."

JEREMIAH 29:11 NIV

"The joy of the LORD is your strength!"

NEHEMIAH 8:10 NLT

But seek ye first the kingdom of God,
and his righteousness; and all these
things shall be added unto you.

MATTHEW 6:33 KJV

Lord, You will cultivate joy within me if I will let You. Then others will see it. My family, my friends—everyone will want You to be their gardener, too. Please let the soil of my heart be fertile for the seeds You want to sow.

Father, I ask for Your power to change. I don't want to be the way I used to be. I want to be wise and enjoy sound thinking. I want to make good decisions in how I express myself in my words and actions.

Help me to be a woman who can keep a secret and not betray a confidence. Help me to be trustworthy in all my conversations, Lord.

Lord, I thank You for my salvation. I thank You for Your indescribable gift of eternal life and the power to do Your will today. I can hardly fathom how You suffered, yet You did it all for me—for every person on this planet. Mocked and beaten, You bled for my sins. You had victory over death so I could live. You made a way for me, and I am eternally grateful.

Father, when I am a poor example to someone I meet, grant me forgiveness. Grant those I offend the wisdom to understand that no one is free of sin, but Your grace is sufficient.

Lord, You give the best gifts! I receive the love gift of my salvation, knowing that it is by grace that I have been saved, through faith. I didn't do anything to deserve it or earn it. I know my works did not save me. Instead, You saved me by grace so I can now do good works to bring glory to Your name.

Lord, You know how painful it is when things are not right between friends. I long for connected relationships, where people live in peace and harmony and there is no resentment between them. What a joy it is to know that I am made right with God by faith. We can communicate freely, talking and listening, enjoying each other as heart friends. I want to live in a growing love relationship with You. Thank You for restoration and righteousness.

Lord, please open my eyes to my own sin, and prevent me from leading my friends astray.

Father, I know my understanding is weak. But when I am in need of guidance, the first place I turn to is Your Word. Help me to search diligently, for I know the answers I need are there.

God, thank You for understanding friends. Thank You that so often we're on the same wavelength, laughing together, crying together, encouraging each other with our understanding.

Lord, the next time I am faced with danger for Your sake, let me remember that You are faithful to reward Your people, no matter how much I may fear.

Lord, please give me the humility
You had when You washed the feet
of the disciples. I am willing to take
on whatever task—high or low—that
You have for me. Grant me the spirit
of cooperation as I work with others.
Show me how to use my gift in new and
different ways. I serve to bring glory
and honor and blessing to You.

Lord, sometimes I feel like my
emotions need a makeover. Renovate
me—transform me, so I can be
balanced and healthy in my emotions.

Lord, I thank You for my wonderful friends! As I think about the treasure chest of my close friends, casual friends, and acquaintances, I am grateful for the blessings and the joys each one brings to my life.

Father, I know those who believe in You will live with You forever. What a blessed thing! I pray that others around the world will hear the message so that they, too, can accept Your gift of eternal life. Show me how I can help spread the message, all to Your glory.

Lord, I humbly bow before You now and confess my sins to You. I am sorry for all of my wrongdoing, and I ask Your forgiveness. I believe Jesus is the Son of God and that He died on a cross and was raised from the dead. He conquered death so that I might really live—in power and purpose here on earth and forever with Him in heaven. I choose You. Please be my Savior and my Lord.

Lord, sometimes compassion is all a person needs to gain strength. I pray I will always offer it freely.

Precious Father, on my own, I am bound to fail. Now that I have put my trust in You, I cannot fail, for You are always the victor, and this knowledge makes me strong where once I was weak.

Lord, help me work to be a blessing to those around me in my daily life.

Times of war are upon us, Father. I ask for Your comfort for all the wives and mothers who sit and wait, no matter on what side their loved ones fight. Thank You for Your consolation and comfort.

Lord, I feel as if my friends are distant and busy. They don't seem to have time for me. Maybe I've been preoccupied, too. I ask that You would bring closer friendships into my life. I need to feel connected. I need their support and encouragement. Show me where I need to reach out more to others. Help me to listen, seek to understand, and offer unconditional love and acceptance—and find the same in return.

Lord, thank You that my friends and I are on Your mind every single day.

There are times, Lord, when I feel as if You've forgotten me. How could I let those feelings of being forsaken overwhelm me? Help me to remember that the Creator of the entire universe holds me in His hands!

Father, fill our hearts full of You and Your Word; then we can sing with grace and joy. My family and I can proclaim Your goodness to all that we meet. What a blessing!

I pray for others with the confidence that You, dear Lord, hear my prayer. That although at times this world seems so unsettled, Your hand is upon our missionaries and pastors, guarding them when they are awake and as they sleep. Give them the strength to do what You have called them to do. Give them the means to help the lost, starving, diseased, and imprisoned. Give them wisdom as they reveal Your Word and reach into the darkness to spread Your light.

Lord, thank You for Your attention to those who struggle, for Your provision, and for the promise that their dreams will eventually come true. I wish them the contentment I am now enjoying.

I'm ashamed to admit that I often speak before I think, and the words that come out of my mouth are anything but wise. Help my children to be wise enough to think first, then speak. Please help me be a good example.

Father, thank You that I am Your child. Remind me each day to count the many blessings You shower upon me, rather than focus on the negatives of this world.

Vows to You must be kept, Father. You not only remember Your promises to us, You never forget our promises to You. Help me treat my vows to You seriously, Lord. If sacrifices are required of me, let me bear them in faith.

I pray against discord and fighting in my family, and I pray for peace. When the challenges of life come, help us to love and support one another with empathy, kindness, and love.

As I look out for the needs of others and not just my own, Father, I pray that I would be a vessel of Your blessing and joy.

Lord, may our home be a place where we show love and respect to one another. Help us to value each member of our family and everyone we welcome into our home. We may not always agree; we may have different opinions. But I pray that we would extend kindness to others and seek to view them as significant, worthy, and valuable. We choose to honor others in our home because we honor You.

*When we were overwhelmed by
sins, you forgave our transgressions.
Blessed are those you choose and bring
near to live in your courts! We are
filled with the good things of your
house, of your holy temple.*

PSALM 65:3–4 NIV

*You come to the help of those
who gladly do right, who
remember your ways.*

ISAIAH 64:5 NIV

*Praise be to the God and Father
of our Lord Jesus Christ, who has
blessed us in the heavenly realms with
every spiritual blessing in Christ.
For he chose us in him before the
creation of the world to be holy
and blameless in his sight.*

EPHESIANS 1:3–4 NIV

Father, as long as I trust in Your presence, I have nothing to worry about. Nothing can separate me from You, because You are the strong Protector, the mighty One who watches over me always. I praise You, Lord, for Your protection.

Lord, forgive me when I treat my family members poorly. Show me their good points, for I have overlooked or forgotten many of them. For the sake of our parents, our children, and ourselves, help me bring peace, forgiveness, and love to our family.

Thank You, Jesus, for Your sacrificial love for me. Thank You for the example of true love that You have provided.

Lord, there are many forces in the world that are coming against my children and me. Your Word says that there is nothing in heaven or on earth that can separate us from Your love. Thank You for Your wonderful reassurance.

Holy Spirit, I pray for a hedge of protection around our home and family. Lord, we look to You as our refuge, our strength, and our security.

Lord, I am truly amazed at Your great power. By the power of God, Jesus was raised from the dead. And You will raise me, too. You lift my spirits from sadness to joy. You give me energy when my kids have depleted me. You help me find funds when my car needs repair. You give me friends to encourage me and to share my life with. You heal bodies and broken relationships. Thank You for the power to live this life every day.

Father, help me to be a faithful, loving, and unforgettable friend.

Lord, I need an attitude adjustment that can only come from You. Let me be a cheerful worker. Resolve my conflicted feelings, and give me Your peace.

Lord, I thank You for the joy of celebration! Help us to be a family that remembers and gathers together—not just for birthdays and holidays but even to celebrate the little blessings of life.

Lord, as I read and study Your Word and hear sermons preached about it, I still have questions and much to learn. I ask that You give me a clear understanding of what You are saying to me through it.

God, I want to have relationships that
are true and honest. Help me to tell the
truth in the most gentle and positive
way. I want my friends to know the
truth about me and about the things
that concern them. When they ask
my advice, help me to share truth and
wisdom from You that will help them
grow in their relationship with You.
Show them that I love them and
want Your best for their lives.

Lord, when times are hard and I become discouraged, be with me. Keep me a faithful teacher of the Way for the sake of my children and all those to come.

Through Your Spirit, Lord, may I show I care about my friends. Give me wisdom to know when my ears should be open and my mouth shut.

God, thank You for giving me good girlfriends. Help me to be a sister in Christ with each and every one of my friends and to spend time cultivating our relationship in You.

I think my best friend is a lot like You, Lord. She offers me spiritual encouragement; she's there for me in the happy times and the sad; and she'd do anything for me. How could I not love her? People of her nature are like precious pearls. I'm so blessed to have her—and You!—in my life.

Lord, I know not all prayers are answered, but many are, so I continue to petition You, for You are my hope.

Dear Lord, help me choose my friends wisely so that I will be positively influenced.

Lord, I thank You for the wisdom You give me each day to watch over the affairs of my household. Give me energy to accomplish my work and to keep our home organized and running smoothly. Help me to be a good time manager and to stay centered on Your purposes. I need to get my tasks done, but I also want to nurture and cherish my relationships. Empower me, Lord. Help our home to be a place of order, peace, and enjoyment.

Lord, help me to make friends with people who like me for me. Don't let me fall into the trap of trying to win friends by doing things that will entertain or please them. Help me to be a leader and not a follower. The only one I want to please is You.

Father, there comes a time in every woman's life when her parents begin to need help. Give me the wisdom to understand the problems they are having and the often simple ways I can be of service to them.

Lord, You created us to be sensitive to the effects of words. Please give me the wisdom to liberally sprinkle the flavor of graciousness into my speech.

Lord Jesus, You have paid for my salvation through Your death on the cross. You made me a child of light that I might guide others to You. You have made me worthy, and I thank You.

I am proud of my children, Lord, but I don't want this pride to be wicked or foolish; rather, let it be the motherly type that is based on unconditional love.

Today in anger, I said something
I shouldn't have. Forgive me, Lord.
Instead of speaking in anger and
frustration, I want to fill my mouth
with words of continual praise to You.

I pray for Your bright, shining light to
spread out into the world. For Your
love to reach the ends of the earth.
Give comfort to those who suffer from
abuse and violence. Touch them with
Your healing light and guard them
with Your protective hand. Give them
assurance that You are there. Allow
them to feel Your presence, hear
Your voice, feel Your touch.

All men and women are equal in Your sight, Father. Jesus died for every one of us, no matter where we come from or what color our skin is. Help me not to value one relationship over another because of influence, wealth, intellect, or race. Help me to see others from Your perspective, no matter how different other people are from me. Help me to love them and learn from the differences we have.

Lord, so many times I am tempted to think that people or things will satisfy me. But often they leave me empty and unfulfilled. Help me to remember that You are the Source of my hope—not a man, or a better job, or a pan of brownies. Those are all good things, but they will never fully satisfy me like You do. Forgive me for misplaced hope. Help me to put my trust in You and Your secure, steady, and unfailing love.

Father, give me Your peace and an understanding that all things work together for good when I follow Your will.

Father, I need to show my children how important obedience is by being obedient myself—to You and to others in authority over me. Thank You for assisting me in this effort.

Lord, may those I work with always see You in my life and be brought closer to You through me.

Dear God, thank You for the new friends You send into my life. Help me never to think I have all the friends I need. Remind me that You have new ways to touch me through each person that I meet.

Lord, thank You for Your promise to guide me in all things, great and small. Your eye is always on me, keeping me from error and ensuring that I can always find a way home to You.

Father, help me to get over self-doubt.
Remind me that Your blessings are
forever and I have nothing to fear. Give
me a merry heart.

I pray for Your power to sustain me
as I take care of myself—by eating
healthy food, drinking enough water,
and making movement and exercise a
part of my daily life. Give me the self-
control and motivation I need to make
wise choices to support the health
of my mind, my spirit, and my body.
Please keep me from injury and illness,
and keep me safe, I pray.

Lord, I want to help bring others to You, to be judged a virtuous woman for Your sake, not for any glory that might come to me. Use me as You see fit, because any work You give me is an honor.

Forgive me, Lord, for those times when I've doubted Your love. Let me close my eyes, hold out my hand, and know that You are there. Thank You for being with me, Father.

Lord, help my children to dedicate themselves to serving You in whatever capacity You would call them.

Your hands made me and formed me;
give me understanding to learn
your commands.

PSALM 119:73 NIV

Your kingdom is an everlasting
kingdom, and your dominion endures
through all generations. The LORD is
trustworthy in all he promises and
faithful in all he does.

PSALM 145:13 NIV

"Teach me, and I will be quiet;
show me where I have been wrong."

JOB 6:24 NIV

Your Word is my daily nourishment,
Lord. Thank You for the Bread of Life
You provide every single day. Those
words feed and nurture my soul just as
eating bread fills me and provides the
nutrition I need to live. Without Your
words I will fade and die spiritually;
with them I am vibrant, energized,
and alive! Be my portion, Lord, as I
seek You. And not just Your hands and
what You give but also Your face, Lord.
I desire to know who You really are.

Father, the life I am living right now is not the result of my faith in You but of Your faith in me. Thank You for Your sacrifice that saves me and makes me whole.

Lord, help me overcome the urge to pat myself on the back in the sight of others, and instead to wait to hear You say, "Well done."

Guard my life, and rescue me, Father. Help me to take refuge in You.

Lord, sometimes I have been targeted by the misguided missiles of well-meaning friends. Show me that true relief is spelled J-E-S-U-S.

God, through the divine power of Your Spirit and Your Word, I pray for my neighborhood. Demolish the stronghold of evil within this community. Touch each heart with Your peace and understanding. You know what each family needs. Help me to be an encouragement to them. Be with me as I take a prayer walk around this neighborhood, lifting each family up to Your heavenly throne.

Lord, I want to love the way You do. I want to be strong, to lovingly discipline my children so they will grow to be pleasing to You. No matter how difficult it is, I will chastise with love.

Lord, I thank You for Your words that speak to my heart and needs. I long to soak in Your teaching and learn more about You. Your life-giving messages are like rain showers on new green grass. I need not just a sprinkle but a downpour—a soaking, abundant rain in my dry heart!

Father, give me the courage and
strength to reach out to all people and
to make new friends.

*Lord, Your Word is a lamp in my
darkness—a flashlight on the path of
life that helps me see the way. Your
words enlighten me with wisdom,
insight, and hope, even when I cannot
see where I am going or how things
will turn out. I'm so glad that You
know the right direction. You have
gone before me and are always with
me, so I don't need to be afraid. I
choose to follow Your leading.*

Lord, thank You for the promise of giving and receiving. Help me to bless others as You have blessed me.

I feel like I've been praying forever for a situation that does not seem to be changing, Lord. I feel like Job: Here I am on my knees in prayer while the entire world dissolves around me. But I know that You are in control. You know all things. So once again, I lift my concern up to You, confident that You will handle the situation in Your timing.

Dear God, help me to forgive my friends when they seem to let me down. Remind me that only You are perfect; only You can always be there and always understand me.

God, today I lift up the world leaders. Give them wisdom, give them courage, give them minds of peace. There is so much death and destruction in this world, and at times I feel disheartened. But I know where to turn—to You, my Father, who makes all things right.

Thank You, Lord, that Your Word is true. Sometimes it's hard to discern truth from a lie, or from the half-truths that bombard me daily from television, radio, magazines, and popular culture. I want to know the truth and live it. Help me to look to Your steady and solid Word, not to this world, for my life instruction manual. I thank You that You will never lead me astray, that You never lie to me, and that You always keep Your promises.

Lord, I want my house to be Your house—a house of prayer, a place of comfort and peace, a refuge to those in need. Help me make our home a blessing for all who pass through its door.

Dear Lord, You parted the Red Sea, and You still the wind and the waves. You give sight to the blind and hearing to the deaf. You raise people from the dead. Your power is awesome. Nothing is impossible for You. I bow before You, singing praises to Your name.

Lord, I'm grateful that I'm not alone, that I can share my life with my friends. And when I listen to them, give me a heart that understands.

Father, I get discouraged when I don't know which way to go. Remind me that You are right behind me, telling me which way to turn. Help me to be quiet and listen for Your guidance.

Father, You hold the universe in Your hands, and yet You are concerned with everything going on in my life. I am staggered by Your love and faithfulness to me.

Lord, if there is one thing I need, it's trustworthy guidance. In darkness or light, on fair days or foul, I trust that the light of Your Word will bring me safely home.

Lord, I long to be more connected to You. Teach me to worship You as the true source of power and love. I adore You like no other. Teach me to pray. Change me, Lord. Transform me so my prayers will be powerful and my life will be fruitful. And may all that I do bring glory to Your name.

Dear Lord, thank You for the gift of friendship. Through this gift You have given me love, comfort, laughter, and countless blessings. Help me to show my friends how much they mean to me. Help me to always look to You for guidance as I hold these delicate relationships in my heart and hands.

Lord, show me my errors, and teach me the proper way to take advice.

God, I want relationships that will bring me closer to You. Help me to choose the healthy relationships that keep me accountable in my daily walk with You.

Lord, thank You for every blessing, both big and small. Help me to be more aware of the ways in which You take care of me, so my gratitude can continue to grow.

Lord, I humble myself before You, bowing down at Your throne. You are so great, so awesome. Your presence fills this universe. I am filled with Your amazing love, touched by Your compassion. There is no one like You in my life, my Master, my Lord, my God.

My Shepherd, my Lord, my Savior, lead me beside the still waters. Lie with me in the green pastures. Restore my soul. Lead me down the paths of Your choosing today. With You by my side, I fear no evil. You are my Comfort and my Guide. I am happy in Your presence. Your goodness and Your mercy are with me this minute, this hour, and this day.

O God, finding friends who glorify You can be difficult. Help me to please You and find other godly people, too.

Father, I know it is Your will for me to understand Your Word, and You have given me the Holy Spirit to guide me. Help me to take advantage of this great blessing.

God, You have done so many things for me, saved me from so many dangers, toils, and snares. I cry out to You again this morning. Fill me with Your Spirit. Touch me with Your presence. And as I go through this day, may I be so filled with Your praises that I cannot help but tell others what You have done for me!

When I consider thy heavens, the work of thy fingers, the moon and the stars, which thou hast ordained; what is man, that thou art mindful of him? and the son of man, that thou visitest him? For thou hast made him a little lower than the angels, and hast crowned him with glory and honour.

PSALM 8:3–5 KJV

Teach us to number our days, that we may gain a heart of wisdom. Satisfy us in the morning with your unfailing love, that we may sing for joy and be glad all our days.

PSALM 90:12, 14 NIV

*F*orever, Lord—what encouragement
is in that word. We have all eternity to
spend with You in heaven. Thank You
for this indescribable gift. Thank You
for being the Alpha and the Omega,
the first and the last.

*My heart rejoices in Your presence!
To Your ears, Lord, I pray that my
singing will be a joyful noise. Your
grace is amazing. You are my all in all;
I worship and adore You. Lean down
Your ear to me as I sing about Your
love, for how great Thou art, Lord!
How great Thou art!*

Lord, guard my tongue as I teach my children. Season my speech with grace—to encourage my children and remind them to walk in Your path.

Lord, help me to be real with those You have put around me. I pray that they see You through me and it draws them closer to You.

Father, please protect my children from spiritual and physical harm, and give them sound minds and bodies. I thank You in advance for answered prayers.

Lord, guide me daily to commit to being perfect. I know I can't expect my family to be perfect if I'm not willing to set the example. Help me as I strive to be like You.

I praise You, Father, for providing green pastures, places to relax and unwind in the Spirit. Please still my heart from distractions, and be the restorer of my soul.

Thank You, Lord. You have given me a wonderful example of patient endurance. When I am losing patience with my children, I recall how long You waited for me to repent and turn to You.

Father God, though Your strength is limitless, it's tempered with wisdom and gentleness. You are both my strong tower and my tender, loving Father. Help me to find that proper balance of gentle strength in my own life.

Father, on my worst days I feel totally unworthy. But I know You have promised to cleanse me from all unrighteousness, to wipe away my guilt and make me whole if I confess my sins.

Lord, please help me to make a priority of eating a nutritious blend of foods, to drink enough water, and to avoid overindulging in junk food.

Father, help me to make the people in my life feel loved and cherished. Help me to remember that I am a letter from You as I interact with others.

Lord, I know I can't hope to escape every unpleasant circumstance in this world. Just the same, I will trust in You, whatever comes. Protect me in the way You see fit, in the way that best advances Your purpose for my life.

Lord, I need rest. I pray that I will sleep well at night. I ask for more energy during the day and a more vibrant spirit.

Father, every day is a battle. I struggle between following You and choosing what feels right at the moment. I need Your wisdom and power to persevere toward a true change of heart and action. But, most of all, I need Your forgiveness.

Lord, life seems overwhelming to me sometimes. Please help me to relax in the knowledge that You will guide me.

Lord, I want to keep my mind healthy and active. Give me wisdom regarding what I put into my mind. I need to feed it the right things so I can be alert and self-controlled.

Lord, let my home be a comforting haven for my family and friends. May it be a place where they can momentarily escape the pressures of this world. Help me to do my best to make it a place where people will know they are loved by me and, more importantly, by You.

Lord, there are many times when I need You and Your Word to guide me. Lead me, and help me become an overcomer.

Help me invest my time in more worthy pursuits, Lord—ones that will provide lasting satisfaction. I'm not sure what You will ask of me, but I am willing to try anything You recommend and give any resulting praise to You.

Lord, when it comes to courage,
I have none of my own. Without You,
I would be filled with fear, terrified
of a future I cannot see. Thank You
for patiently taking my hand and
helping me face my fears.

Lord, remind me of Your presence throughout the day. Help me to reflect Your Son, Jesus Christ.

When I grow old, Lord, I pray that I will see the fruits of my labor and rejoice, knowing that all my efforts were well worth the time and energy I put into them.

Lord, I would prefer to live a life of peace, but when I must fight for those I love, I pray You will give me the strength to do so.

*Hide your face from my sins and
blot out all my iniquity. Create in me
a pure heart, O God, and renew
a steadfast spirit within me.*

PSALM 51:9–10 NIV

*Open my eyes that I may see
wonderful things in your law.*

PSALM 119:18 NIV

*Teach me knowledge and good
judgment, for I trust your commands.*

PSALM 119:66 NIV

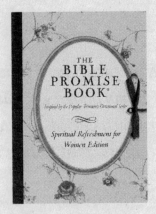